FOURTH GRADE MATH WORKBOOK

DECIMALS MADE EASY

BABY PROFESSOR
EDUCATION KIDS

Speedy Publishing LLC
40 E. Main St. #1156
Newark, DE 19711
www.speedypublishing.com

DECIMAL ADDITION

Decimal addition - 1 digit - LEVEL 1

1. 0.9 + 0.9 = _____

2. 1.1 + 1.7 = _____

3. 2.3 + 1.3 = _____

4. 2.1 + 1.1 = _____

5. 0.3 + 1.4 = _____

6. 2.2 + 0.3 = _____

7. 1.6 + 0.4 = _____

8. 0.2 + 0.7 = _____

9. 2.7 + 1.5 = _____

10. 1.3 + 1.1 = _____

11. 0.3 + 0.0 = _____

12. 2.2 + 0.8 = _____

13. 2.6 + 0.4 = _____

14. 1.1 + 0.7 = _____

15. 2.1 + 1.8 = _____

16. 1.0 + 1.7 = _____

17. 1.1 + 0.2 = _____

18. 1.4 + 1.7 = _____

19. 1.5 + 0.6 = _____

20. 2.4 + 1.9 = _____

21. 2.5 + 0.4 = _____

22. 1.6 + 0.5 = _____

23. 1.6 + 1.4 = _____

24. 1.9 + 0.2 = _____

25. 2.1 + 0.8 = _____

26. 0.1 + 1.7 = _____

27. 0.2 + 0.4 = _____

28. 0.4 + 0.9 = _____

29. 1.8 + 0.7 = _____

30. 0.0 + 1.5 = _____

31. 2.2 + 0.2 = _____

32. 1.7 + 1.6 = _____

33. 1.7 + 1.9 = _____

34. 1.3 + 1.0 = _____

35. 0.2 + 0.2 = _____

36. 2.0 + 1.7 = _____

37. 2.9 + 1.3 = _____

38. 2.5 + 1.9 = _____

Decimal addition - 1 digit - LEVEL 2

1. 3.8 + 4.6 = ______

2. 4.5 + 2.0 = ______

3. 6.6 + 0.2 = ______

4. 6.0 + 7.5 = ______

5. 7.5 + 8.2 = ______

6. 7.4 + 1.4 = ______

7. 7.9 + 5.1 = ______

8. 9.7 + 6.7 = ______

9. 1.0 + 5.7 = ______

10. 3.2 + 10.2 = ______

11. 1.9 + 6.4 = ______

12. 1.1 + 1.9 = ______

13. 7.0 + 7.4 = ______

14. 7.2 + 3.7 = ______

15. 8.8 + 1.8 = ______

16. 9.3 + 2.7 = ______

17. 6.7 + 3.5 = ______

18. 4.5 + 4.6 = ______

19. 8.6 + 9.0 = ______

20. 7.4 + 6.2 = ______

21. 9.7 + 1.6 = ______

22. 1.9 + 4.5 = ______

23. 0.8 + 0.2 = ______

24. 7.8 + 2.8 = ______

25. 9.1 + 8.8 = ______

26. 7.9 + 0.5 = ______

27. 8.5 + 0.4 = ______

28. 7.6 + 2.7 = ______

29. 2.7 + 9.6 = ______

30. 8.3 + 6.6 = ______

31. 3.2 + 9.6 = ______

32. 1.3 + 7.2 = ______

33. 0.2 + 1.7 = ______

34. 5.2 + 0.9 = ______

35. 4.3 + 4.1 = ______

36. 4.1 + 8.4 = ______

37. 6.7 + 0.3 = ______

38. 4.9 + 4.4 = ______

39. 3.3 + 2.4 = ______

40. 7.2 + 0.3 = ______

Decimal addition - 1 digit + 2 digit - LEVEL 3

1. 0.1 + 0.9 = ______

2. 0.3 + 0.5 = ______

3. 0.9 + 1.7 = ______

4. 0.03 + 0.1 = ______

5. 1.3 + 1.6 = ______

6. 0.9 + 1.3 = ______

7. 0.2 + 1.69 = ______

8. 1.6 + 1.6 = ______

9. 1.5 + 0.7 = ______

10. 1.29 + 1.9 = ______

11. 1.1 + 1.34 = ______

12. 0.4 + 0.07 = ______

13. 1.3 + 1.9 = ______

14. 1.0 + 0.0 = ______

15. 0.70 + 1.3 = ______

16. 1.14 + 0.5 = ______

17. 1.6 + 0.8 = ______

18. 1.5 + 0.5 = ______

19. 0.9 + 1.6 = ______

20. 0.0 + 1.1 = ______

21. 0.31 + 0.6 = ______

22. 0.3 + 1.11 = ______

23. 1.9 + 0.4 = ______

24. 1.5 + 1.0 = ______

25. 0.3 + 0.1 = ______

26. 1.2 + 0.58 = ______

27. 0.77 + 1.3 = ______

28. 1.05 + 1.7 = ______

29. 0.1 + 1.37 = ______

30. 1.5 + 0.1 = ______

31. 1.4 + 1.85 = ______

32. 0.1 + 0.5 = ______

33. 1.4 + 1.4 = ______

34. 1.3 + 1.53 = ______

35. 1.2 + 0.31 = ______

36. 1.4 + 0.8 = ______

37. 0.9 + 0.2 = ______

38. 1.7 + 1.2 = ______

39. 1.3 + 0.6 = ______

40. 0.82 + 1.2 = ______

Decimal addition - 1 or 2 digits - LEVEL 4

1. 1.0 + 0.0 = ______

2. 1.54 + 0.80 = ______

3. 0.03 + 1.8 = ______

4. 0.74 + 0.7 = ______

5. 1.79 + 0.43 = ______

6. 0.3 + 1.49 = ______

7. 0.4 + 0.80 = ______

8. 0.7 + 1.14 = ______

9. 1.5 + 1.54 = ______

10. 1.5 + 1.8 = ______

11. 0.91 + 0.81 = ______

12. 0.3 + 0.9 = ______

13. 0.10 + 0.80 = ______

14. 0.7 + 0.9 = ______

15. 0.16 + 1.2 = ______

16. 0.80 + 0.84 = ______

17. 1.42 + 0.0 = ______

18. 0.07 + 1.90 = ______

19. 1.46 + 1.5 = ______

20. 0.85 + 1.16 = ______

21. 1.31 + 1.03 = ______

22. 0.4 + 0.8 = ______

23. 1.7 + 0.31 = ______

24. 0.25 + 1.1 = ______

25. 1.5 + 1.4 = ______

26. 1.9 + 0.89 = ______

27. 1.7 + 0.83 = ______

28. 1.85 + 0.49 = ______

29. 1.7 + 0.2 = ______

30. 1.0 + 0.2 = ______

31. 0.50 + 0.5 = ______

32. 1.2 + 0.9 = ______

33. 1.15 + 0.60 = ______

34. 1.56 + 0.83 = ______

35. 1.19 + 1.36 = ______

36. 1.7 + 1.08 = ______

37. 1.6 + 1.98 = ______

38. 0.95 + 1.7 = ______

39. 0.2 + 1.9 = ______

40. 0.70 + 0.25 = ______

DECIMAL SUBTRACTION

Decimal subtraction - 1 digit - LEVEL 1

1. 3.4 – 2.4 = ______

2. 5.5 – 2.3 = ______

3. 8.6 – 0.8 = ______

4. 0.5 – 0.1 = ______

5. 4.6 – 4.3 = ______

6. 2.1 – 0.0 = ______

7. 4.5 – 0.7 = ______

8. 5.7 – 2.2 = ______

9. 0.6 – 0.3 = ______

10. 5.3 – 4.6 = ______

11. 4.6 – 1.0 = ______

12. 10.8 – 2.0 = ______

13. 5.0 – 1.5 = ______

14. 9.6 – 2.4 = ______

15. 8.5 – 4.4 = ______

16. 3.7 – 1.4 = ______

17. 1.2 – 0.1 = ______

18. 5.2 – 4.3 = ______

19. 2.5 – 2.5 = ______

20. 6.9 – 5.8 = ______

21. 3.7 – 0.8 = ______

22. 10.9 – 2.9 = ______

23. 10.3 – 4.0 = ______

24. 9.2 – 2.8 = ______

25. 4.9 – 2.7 = ______

26. 5.8 – 3.8 = ______

27. 3.1 – 2.2 = ______

28. 7.4 – 5.1 = ______

29. 10.6 – 3.4 = ______

30. 5.8 – 4.2 = ______

31. 1.9 – 0.5 = ______

32. 6.0 – 0.0 = ______

33. 8.7 – 2.9 = ______

34. 10.3 – 3.2 = ______

35. 2.8 – 1.5 = ______

36. 9.4 – 2.1 = ______

37. 5.0 – 2.2 = ______

38. 3.7 – 1.0 = ______

Decimal subtraction - 1 digit - LEVEL 2

1. 0.4 – 0.4 = ______

2. 9.5 – 1.8 = ______

3. 4.7 – 0.0 = ______

4. 1.8 – 1.24 = ______

5. 9.8 – 1.5 = ______

6. 4.1 – 1.9 = ______

7. 2.1 – 1.7 = ______

8. 5.86 – 1.5 = ______

9. 5.65 – 1.9 = ______

10. 7.0 – 1.0 = ______

11. 2.47 – 0.8 = ______

12. 4.02 – 0.6 = ______

13. 9.03 – 1.0 = _______

20. 10.4 – 1.3 = _______

14. 2.9 – 0.1 = _______

21. 8.91 – 0.0 = _______

15. 8.6 – 1.7 = _______

22. 4.33 – 1.8 = _______

16. 1.5 – 0.12 = _______

23. 6.17 – 1.1 = _______

17. 3.27 – 0.3 = _______

24. 3.0 – 1.1 = _______

18. 1.9 – 1.6 = _______

25. 3.5 – 0.6 = _______

19. 4.6 – 1.4 = _______

26. 9.8 – 1.0 = _______

27. 10.48 – 1.7 = ________

28. 4.71 – 0.4 = ________

29. 2.10 – 1.9 = ________

30. 10.3 – 0.7 = ________

31. 1.11 – 0.8 = ________

32. 7.66 – 0.0 = ________

33. 10.0 – 1.1 = ________

34. 4.68 – 1.5 = ________

35. 7.65 – 0.7 = ________

36. 5.17 – 1.6 = ________

37. 1.83 – 0.6 = ________

38. 8.8 – 0.0 = ________

39. 2.06 – 1.1 = ________

40. 3.2 – 0.5 = ________

THE MISSING ADDEND

Decimal addition - missing addend

1. ______ + 1.7 = 10.5

2. ______ + 1.1 = 11.7

3. 10.7 + ______ = 12.2

4. 0.5 + ______ = 6.1

5. 4.7 + ______ = 5.2

6. ______ + 7.4 = 8.1

7. ______ + 0.4 = 5.6

8. 1.2 + ______ = 7.3

9. 5.2 + ______ = 7

10. ______ + 1.8 = 4.5

11. 0.8 + ______ = 11.1

12. ______ + 3.4 = 4.6

13. 8.2 + ______ = 8.7

14. ______ + 1.6 = 4.5

15. ______ + 1.4 = 10

16. ______ + 0.1 = 9.4

17. ______ + 1.5 = 4.8

18. ______ + 0.4 = 11

19. 2.7 + ______ = 3.9

20. ______ + 1.5 = 8.9

21. ______ + 8.3 = 10.2

22. 1.9 + ______ = 4.3

23. 3.5 + ______ = 4

24. ______ + 7.0 = 8.7

25. ______ + 9.6 = 9.9

26. 10.4 + ______ = 12.2

27. ______ + 1.9 = 11.2

28. 8.8 + ______ = 9.5

29. ______ + 0.6 = 8.6

30. 0.1 + ______ = 1.9

31. 0.7 + ______ = 3.9

32. ______ + 8.8 = 8.8

33. ______ + 0.6 = 0.8

34. 5.3 + ______ = 6.4

35. 7.5 + ______ = 8.2

36. 3.8 + ______ = 3.8

37. ______ + 7.2 = 8.6

38. 1.5 + ______ = 10.5

THE MISSING MINUEND/ SUBTRAHEND

Decimal addition - missing minuend/subtrahend

1. 7 – ______ = 5.7

2. ______ – 0.4 = 1.6

3. 6 – ______ = 5.3

4. ______ – 0.2 = 0.8

5. ______ – 0.3 = 0.7

6. ______ – 0.4 = 4.6

7. 2 – ______ = 0.1

8. 3.9 – ______ = 3.4

9. ______ – 0.5 = 3.5

10. ______ – 1.5 = 4.5

11. ______ – 0.0 = 0

12. ______ – 1.1 = 7.7

13. ______ – 0.3 = 8

14. 1.8 – ______ = 0.9

15. 3.5 – ______ = 3.4

16. ______ – 1.3 = 5.7

17. ______ – 0.9 = 9.2

18. 3 – ______ = 1.1

19. ______ – 0.3 = 1.1

20. ______ – 0.7 = 8.3

21. ______ – 0.4 = 5.6

22. ______ – 1.3 = 1.7

23. ______ – 1.9 = 5.1

24. ______ – 0.7 = 3

25. ______ − 1 = 0.2

26. ______ − 0.9 = 0.7

27. ______ − 0.9 = 1.2

28. 4.7 − ______ = 2.8

29. 1.7 − ______ = 1.7

30. 7 − ______ = 6.7

31. 6 − ______ = 4.2

32. ______ − 1 = 0.7

33. 1.4 − ______ = 0.4

34. ______ − 0.6 = 0.6

35. 10.9 − ______ = 10

36. 1 − ______ = 0

37. 3 − ______ = 2.3

38. 6.2 − ______ = 5.5

ANSWERS

ADDEND

LEVEL 1

1. 1.8
2. 2.8
3. 3.6
4. 3.2
5. 1.7
6. 2.5
7. 2
8. 0.9
9. 4.2
10. 2.4
11. 0.3
12. 3
13. 3
14. 1.8
15. 3.9
16. 2.7
17. 1.3
18. 3.1
19. 2.1
20. 4.3
21. 2.9
22. 2.1
23. 3
24. 2.1
25. 2.9
26. 1.8
27. 0.6
28. 1.3
29. 2.5
30. 1.5
31. 4.4
32. 3.3
33. 3.6
34. 2.3
35. 0.4
36. 3.7
37. 4.2
38. 4.4

LEVEL 2

1. 8.4
2. 6.5
3. 6.8
4. 13.5
5. 15.7
6. 8.8
7. 13
8. 16.4
9. 6.7
10. 13.4
11. 8.3
12. 3
13. 14.4
14. 10.9
15. 10.6
16. 12
17. 10.2
18. 9.1
19. 17.6
20. 13.6
21. 11.3
22. 6.4
23. 1
24. 10.6
25. 17.9
26. 8.4
27. 8.9

ANSWERS

28. 10.3
29. 12.3
30. 14.9
31. 12.8
32. 8.5
33. 1.9
34. 6.1
35. 8.4
36. 12.5
37. 7
38. 9.3
39. 5.7
40. 7.5

LEVEL 3

1. 1
2. 0.8
3. 2.6
4. 0.13
5. 2.9
6. 2.2
7. 1.89
8. 3.2
9. 2.2
10. 3.19
11. 2.44
12. 0.47
13. 3.2
14. 1
15. 2
16. 1.64
17. 2.4
18. 2
19. 2.5
20. 1.1
21. 0.91
22. 1.41
23. 2.3
24. 2.5
25. 0.4
26. 1.78
27. 2.07
28. 2.75
29. 1.47
30. 1.6
31. 3.25
32. 0.6
33. 2.8
34. 2.83
35. 1.51
36. 2.2
37. 1.1
38. 2.9
39. 1.9
40. 2.02

LEVEL 4

1. 1
2. 2.34
3. 1.83
4. 1.44
5. 2.22
6. 1.79
7. 1.2
8. 1.84
9. 3.04
10. 3.3
11. 1.72
12. 1.2
13. 0.9

ANSWERS

14. 1.6
15. 1.36
16. 1.64
17. 1.42
18. 1.97
19. 2.96
20. 2.01
21. 2.34
22. 1.2
23. 2.01
24. 1.35
25. 2.9
26. 2.79
27. 2.53
28. 2.34
29. 1.9
30. 1.2
31. 1
32. 2.1
33. 1.75
34. 2.39
35. 2.55
36. 2.78
37. 3.58
38. 2.65
39. 2.1
40. 0.95

SUBTRACTION

LEVEL 1

1. 1
2. 3.2
3. 7.8
4. 0.4
5. 0.3
6. 2.1
7. 3.8
8. 3.5
9. 0.3
10. 0.7
11. 3.6
12. 8.8
13. 3.5
14. 7.2
15. 4.1
16. 2.3
17. 1.1
18. 0.9
19. 0
20. 1.1
21. 2.9
22. 8
23. 6.3
24. 6.4
25. 2.2
26. 2
27. 0.9
28. 2.3
29. 7.2
30. 1.6
31. 1.4
32. 6
33. 5.8
34. 7.1
35. 1.3
36. 7.3
37. 2.8
38. 2.7

ANSWERS

LEVEL 2

1. 0
2. 7.7
3. 4.7
4. 0.56
5. 8.3
6. 2.2
7. 0.4
8. 4.36
9. 3.75
10. 6
11. 1.67
12. 3.42
13. 8.03
14. 2.8
15. 6.9
16. 1.38
17. 2.97
18. 0.3
19. 3.2
20. 9.1
21. 8.91
22. 2.53
23. 5.07
24. 1.9
25. 2.9
26. 8.8
27. 8.78
28. 4.31
29. 0.2
30. 9.6
31. 0.31
32. 7.66
33. 8.9
34. 3.18
35. 6.95
36. 3.57
37. 1.23
38. 8.8
39. 0.96
40. 2.7

MISSING ADDEND

1. 8.8
2. 10.6
3. 1.5
4. 5.6
5. 0.5
6. 0.7
7. 5.2
8. 6.1
9. 1.8
10. 2.7
11. 10.3
12. 1.2
13. 0.5
14. 2.9
15. 8.6
16. 9.3
17. 3.3
18. 10.6
19. 1.2
20. 7.4
21. 1.9
22. 2.4
23. 0.5
24. 1.7
25. 0.3

ANSWERS

26. 1.8
27. 9.3
28. 0.7
29. 8.0
30. 1.8
31. 3.2
32. 0.0
33. 0.2
34. 1.1
35. 0.7
36. 0.0
37. 1.4
38. 9.0

MISSING MINUEND/ SUBTRAHEND

1. 1.3
2. 2
3. 0.7
4. 1.0
5. 1
6. 5
7. 1.9
8. 0.5
9. 4
10. 6
11. 0
12. 8.8
13. 8.3
14. 0.9
15. 0.1
16. 7
17. 10.1
18. 1.9
19. 1.4
20. 9
21. 6
22. 3
23. 7
24. 3.7
25. 1.2
26. 1.6
27. 2.1
28. 1.9
29. 0
30. 0.3
31. 1.8
32. 1.7
33. 1
34. 1.2
35. 0.9
36. 1.0
37. 0.7
38. 0.7
39. 8
40. 1.6

www.ingramcontent.com/pod-product-compliance
Lightning Source LLC
LaVergne TN
LVHW060514170826
845677LV00026B/1758

* 9 7 9 8 8 6 9 4 5 1 4 9 1 *